My Lovely,
DARK SKIN

Vanessa Wilson

ISBN: 978-1-4669-2068-2 (e)
ISBN: 978-1-4669-2067-5 (sc)

Trafford rev. 04/16/2012

 www.trafford.com

North America & international
toll-free: 1 888 232 4444 (USA & Canada)
phone: 250 383 6864 ♦ fax: 812 355 4082

Contents

Me

MY NAME IS VANESSA WILSON. I am a prideful 40 year old dark-skinned black woman. When I look at my beautiful dark skin, I am filled with pride. When I look at my skin, I am moved with emotion. The pride and emotion overwhelms me, like an ocean. I'm not as dark as the original ebony hue; but I am dark. I feel like I have been cheated out of some darkness; I should be darker than I am. When I see other people in the black race, I get strength from those other dark-tone faces looking back at me. A few words that come to mind when I see ebony skin: strength, longevity, and perseverance. I am wholly inspired. These faces are familiar and they are comforting. Just hearing the word "black", I picture a strong big, black fist.

Imagine, if you can, a sea of black faces; powerful. When I see one black face, I feel that I am standing on the shoulders of millions of black people. Strength comes in numbers. I am even more inspired when dark faces are present in large quantity.

I was born in Atlanta, Georgia: The Black Mecca. I was born February 26, 1971 at Grady Memorial Hospital. As Atlanta folks say, "I am a Grady baby." Due to the Atlanta child murders in the 1970's, my parents decided to move to Tulsa, Oklahoma. We lived in the vicinity of the murderer. I was born in Georgia and grew up in Oklahoma. We have lived, back and forth, between these two places ever since. I presently reside in Oklahoma. There are a lot of issues facing Black America. This is my observation of Black America. There are a lot of situations, affecting us, that need to be addressed. One of these issues is the dark skin vs. light skin. I thought this issue was diminishing but it appears to be increasing and black women are arguing more than ever.

My Queen

THE PICTURE ON THE FRONT of this book is my Queen. My mother and father are the queen and king of my life. She passed away. When I see my mothers' face, even in my mind's eye, I feel that I am standing on the shoulders of tens of millions. My mother, Brenda Wilson, embodied all of the qualities and characteristics of the traditional black queen. She was an Amazon. She had the traditional black woman's form. Luscious curves upon bountiful luscious curves. She was a shapely, full-figured, heavy-set woman (I wished I had her hips). She had bright, high-yellow skin and her hair was naturally curly, like a poodle's coat.

She was a beautiful free spirit. In every sense of the word, freedom, she expressed herself. She had no limitations. She loved to spread her wings and fly; sky's the limit. My mother loved to fully embrace her womanhood. She was an exhibitionist. My mother did not like to be confined. Her philosophies in life: 1. If you like it, I love it. 2. Throw caution to the wind, life is too short.

She over-indulged in discovering herself; that was her pleasure. My mother believed that only two things mattered in life: God and family (In exactly that order). She gave her all to her family. She never made any decisions, in life, without considering how things would affect her: 1. husband. 2. children (In exactly that order). Unselfishly, she always put herself last on her list.

My mom represents all of my queens. In regards to the traditional black queen, she continued in traditional values that started with her mother. She raised her children with the same principles, in which, she was raised. She was a powerhouse. She had strength, determination, and patience. She did not have the original dark skin of black people. She reflected the present black-American woman because she reflects variation in the black race. Black Americas' color variation is constantly changing. My mom told me that

4

one of my cousins told her that she was white. She used to babysit him. My mom used to babysit anybody's and everybody's baby. My mama loved babies. She liked the sound of a baby crying. She loved any sound of a baby. Of course, she corrected my cousin when he told her she was white. She told me, she said, "Boy, I'm blacker than you." He is very dark-skinned. At the time, he was around 8 years old; so that statement may have confused him. My mother felt that she was as free and entitled as any other woman and her light skin should not diminish that fact, among other people. Someone else may define my mother. I'll simply say, "Okay, my white queen."

This beautiful queen of mine also had her king, my father. His name is Tj Wilson. He represents the traditional black man. His skin was markedly contrasted to his yellow, light-skinned wife. He has very dark black skin. Some people might say that he is so black that he is blue. My mother loved it. My mother loved this black man so much; I remember that she would continuously talk about how much she loved this dark skin. She would lift this dark skin up and praise its beauty, non-stop. I remember she told me one time, "I see blue veins in my legs; I don't want to look over at my man and see blue veins in his legs." She had a natural affinity to this dark skin. Opposites do attract. My father allowed this free spirit to continuously renew herself; to shed her old layers and give rise to consistent new growth. If my father denied my mother anything that she needed, he would hear about it later; as a result, so would I. I never did. Somehow, she always manipulated him into her way of thinking. For him to deny her anything; would be his own demise.

They decided to form a union. To this wedded union, three children were born. Most of what I know about my father, I learned from my mother. My father was rarely around the house, when I was a child. I would often wonder and I would ask my mother, "Where is daddy? When is he coming home?" A few philosophies of my father: 1. I will never accept being treated unfairly by anyone. 2. Give me what you owe me. Give me what I am due. 3. Until I get what is due me, I will stay on the gas.

My father and I have a lot more time to talk now. I asked him why he was not around more when I was little. He explained, "I had to go out and work to provide for my family." I would see him around the house, sporadically. The only time I remember him being around was when it was time to discipline his children. In that capacity, he was like clockwork. He ruled his household with an iron-fist. He is a no-nonsense kind of guy. I am grateful to my father for so many things. The greatest gift he could have given me is my mother. I thank him for making a conscientious choice that brought me this great woman. My dad kept my mom elevated during times of turmoil throughout her life. My dad is the traditional black male: a strong black man that pulls his woman through a storm ensuring that she is not badly weathered, after this storm. That's a sexy trait in a man. At the end of the storm, a man ensures that his woman is "no worse for the wear". Majority of the time, my dad was this storm system. In the end he supported her and she felt secure with him. They worked together as a team.

I'm a dog lover. My whole family loves dogs. The family dog was Beau, a boxer; he was not at all attractive but he was cute. He looked menacing; his bark was worse than his bite. We've had other dogs. I like the German shepherd we had; he was a slim, sleek dog. His name was Byron. He was trained and aggressive; I like aggressive dogs. My mom's favorite color was canary yellow. My favorite color is hunter green; I like yellow and then blue. I'm not a cat fan. Once, my mom decided to get a house cat, to counteract the mice. Even though the cat was in the house, he wasn't welcomed. My mom basically took care of the cat because we wouldn't go near it. That cat was a hustling cat. My mom would feed it, frequently, but that cat had to work for extra food; he would pounce on any bird entering the yard. I liked this one cat. I think our cats name was Mickey.

My mom was born in Atlanta, Georgia; and my dad was born in Morris, Oklahoma. My mom preferred the Oklahoma countryside. She loved the Oklahoma blue sky. She said it was different from Georgia's sky. She liked everything about country living. She loved the small towns, slow traffic, and slower living. She liked to ride in the country and take in the scenery. She told me that when she first came to Oklahoma, she smelled something that penetrated her senses. She asked my dad, "What is that great smell?" My dad said, "That's a skunk." Initially, my mother loved the smell of skunks. As the years passed, I think that skunk-smell love faded.

My mom gave me advice about men. One of the things she told me, "Vanessa, when you allow a man to come into your life, you take the whole man; the whole man as he is. This man cannot be broken down into parts. You can't try to divide the man into pieces that you like and pieces that you don't like. I like certain characteristics but I don't like others'. I'll take these qualities but I will try to work on getting rid of his characteristics that I don't like." It means accepting this man as he is and supporting him completely. Stand by your man. All women are going to refine their man. At her meticulous direction, she encouraged her husband to shed his old layers while they both continued to grow together.

My sister, Torie, is 2 years older than me. My brother, Tj, is four years younger than I am. Both of them have a lighter complexion than me. My mother came to me one day and she asked, "Vanessa, do I treat you any differently than I do my light-skinned children?" I couldn't believe that she even had to ask. Did she not think she did her job well? This woman was always doting on blackness. She talked about my father's skin all the time, as well as mine. Initially, I didn't answer her question. I asked my mom, "Who told you that?" She responded, "One of your relatives told me that I treat you differently than my two light-skinned children." I asked again, "Who?" She said, "That's not important." She stood there looking at me, waiting for an answer. I stood there looking at her, waiting for an answer, also. She appeared to be irritated, like she couldn't wait another second for me to answer her. I said, "No mama. Whoever told you that, don't know what they are talking about." We carried on with talking about whatever we were discussing. As I reflect on that time, it was probably a good idea for my mom not to tell me about this particular relative. I was mad. How dare anyone put their insane thoughts or ideas into my mother's head. I cringe when I think of my mom doubting herself; especially when it was about something so unnecessary and unwarranted. I would have told them, "That's your hang-up, my mother loves dark skin." My relative is the one who has issues about being dark black. Yes, it was a good idea for my mother not to tell me about this relative. I'll bet this relative was a female. After all these years, I still haven't let that anger go. Sometimes, I have a hard time letting things go. I'm going to let that anger go.

If truth be told, I should have explained to my mother that she did treat her dark skin child differently than she treated her light-skinned children. I felt like my mom did not acknowledge my two light-skinned siblings. I never heard my mom talk about how beautiful their skin was. I always felt as if they were missing something because they had light-skin. Maybe that's not the correct description. I felt like they were not as privileged. It was a blessing to have dark skin and they didn't have that blessing so I thought they missed something special. Now, I realize that my two other siblings did not need this attention focused on their skin.

They are more socially acceptable to mainstream society. Society would determine what is acceptable and what is beautiful. Encouragement starts at home. My mom would bombard me with these positive confirmations and she always connected these positive affirmations with my black skin. By her combining my positive development with my black skin, I thought my accomplishments were attributed to my black skin. I think it happened on a subconscious level.

When I would make good grades in school; in my mind, the reason I made good grades is because I'm a smart, black girl. When I participated in organized sports; I was successful because I was a skilled, black girl. I'm compassionate about other people because I am a loving, black girl. I am a freedom fighter; you would expect nothing less from a black girl. My mother did a number on me. She had me thinking black was the thing to be; I still do. I am pretty because of my black face; not in spite of my black face. I'm writing these thoughts on paper and I attribute it to my dark skin. Who would I be without this attached black face?

In hindsight, my mother always told me that she did not treat her children the same. If we were the same people then she would treat us the same. We were different people with different needs. One child may need something different from the other child. One child may need more, of something, than the other child. She always spoke positively about this rich, dark skin; I never heard her mention any negative statements. She knew that her dark-skinned daughter would need this build-up. She knew I had to feel proud of my color. Who else would keep me lifted, if not her? Provide what your children need and make the necessary adjustments.

My mother loved her own skin. She could also appreciate other peoples' beauty. I wonder if I could have learned to appreciate my blackness from any other woman. What qualifies this light-skinned woman to educate me about the pride of black skin? What does she know about it? All it takes is love. Her love qualified her to give me everything I needed and that same love kept her focused on what I may need in the future.

I've never had issues about my black skin. I've had other people tell me that I am a pretty black girl. Others around me, people of different races, helped to boost my confidence with nice compliments. Building self-esteem and self-value begins at home. Compliments, from the outside world, were great but they were too few and far in-between to maintain that confidence, at the critical required level. My mother kept me lifted but she couldn't always be with me. I had to stay lifted as I interacted with the outside world. When others were not able to sustain me, with compliments; I would tell myself how amazing I was. The world can be cruel. Negativity comes in all forms. I had to keep myself lifted; if other people could not contribute, I would praise my own beauty. I had to get my fill. I could not wait on other people to pull me up. I had to keep myself pulled up, until others' were able to help; if they could never help, then it didn't matter anyway. I would praise myself enough to make up for what other people didn't provide. I provided it for myself. I made sure that I was completely full and nourished. I try not to think negative thoughts about myself. Sometimes, I'm unsuccessful at it; negative thoughts creep up in my mind.

I've heard that for each negative thought, it takes 28 positive thoughts or statements to override the one negative. I heard this early, in my school years, so it must be a scientific fact. Anytime I was faced with obstacles and barriers, in my life, I would practice this technique. Negative statements have such a powerful impact and they are long-lasting. It takes too much work to overcome negative thoughts. My advice is to leave negative thoughts. You start to believe the things you tell yourself. If you tell yourself negative things then you will believe that about yourself. If you tell yourself positive things then you will believe that about yourself. Even if, at first, you don't believe the positive thoughts; keep repeating them to yourself. You will start to believe them; especially, the more often you repeat them to yourself.

Throughout the course of life, I would come into contact with negative people. Negative people are all around, no matter where you are. It seems like these pessimistic people seek you out, to target you. They pursue you, in an effort, to draw all of the life's energy out of you. They are persistent at their mission. During my childhood years, I would see them all the time, especially in high school. Kids will be kids. Boys were always telling me I was ugly. A boy would say to me, "You're ugly." I would think, "Oh no, a negative comment. Hurry, I would immediately tell myself 28 positive statements. Quickly, before it started to set within my bones." I got to 15 great things about me and another boy would come from nowhere and say, "You're ugly." So, not only did I have to tell myself the other 13 things I didn't get to finish; I had to add 28 more positives, to make up for the last boy. That's a total of 41 wonderful things about me. Negative kids kept me working in high school. High school was a challenging period for me. I told myself the 41 wonderful things; whew, I was all better.

As an adult, I would see these pessimistic people in the workplace. They would do everything to discourage my productive development. They were just determined to ruin my day. I wouldn't let them. I told myself 28 awesome things about Vanessa. I noticed that, as an adult, the positive thoughts come more quickly and easily. Practice makes perfect. That's right girl; shake 'em off. I continued on with my day, fortified.

Now that I look back on things and reminisce about my childhood; I never needed to ask my mother "if father was coming home." Actually, it was something I could have predicted. All I had to do was look for my sister or my brother, and gage what they were doing. If my sister or brother were doing anything requiring disciplinary action; miraculously, out-of-the-blue, my father would appear. Proudly, he showed up for duty.

It was very difficult for me to grow up in this family. I am the middle child. Actually, I am the baby of the family. My sister is the oldest daughter and my brother is an only son. So, that makes me the baby of the group. I used to be quiet, shy, and timid. There was no time to hone those nice, little subtleties in this family. If you wanted to survive in this family, you would have to acquire a more aggressive personality; you would have to develop thicker skin. There was one of two choices: you toughen up or you get ran over.

As children, we all used to fight. I used to beat up my sister and my brother. I used to choke them, both. My sister was older than me but I was always bigger than her. I always used to get the best of her. Once, she got me good. One day we were fighting, she picked up the cable box or telephone and hit me in the head with it. It broke and we couldn't use it. I don't quite remember what hit me (maybe there was some permanent damage). Whatever we broke, my mom was threatening to tell our dad on us. Eventually, when my sister was in high school, my dad kicked her out of the house. I used to choke my brother too. One day we were fighting; he was around 12 or 13 years old. I was trying to get the best of him, like I always do; for the first time, he was overpowering me. I grabbed a candlestick holder and stabbed him with it. I got upset because I could no longer handle him. He wasn't badly hurt, just a scratch. After that, I left him alone.

My siblings were always doing something that would draw my father's attention. It seems they wanted to have him around all the time. Each of my siblings had their own unique personalities. My sister had her challenges, during our up-bringing. Usually, when she got in trouble, it centered around boys. I noticed that she liked to maneuver around, at her leisure. She wanted to be a grown teenager. My father was in direct opposition to this behavior. My father believed that if his children were maneuvering around in society; especially his teenage daughters, he needed to remain abreast of every move they made. Number one rule: If you leave this house, I need to know where you are going. If you go one place and decide to go somewhere else; simply call to keep me aware of your doings and location. You may decide to go to 10 different locations; my father needed to know of each move, before you navigate.

To say the least, my sister had great difficulty mastering this discipline. I think she tried, somehow, but she just couldn't quite get it right. Maybe she would start off on the right track; somewhere during the course of her day, it would all fall apart. She would leave the house and be away, all day long. If she had pre-planned activities, she would notify my parents ahead of time. I think her problems occurred from unexpected events. Perhaps, she ran into some friends and changed her plans on the spot. Although my parents knew about the pre-planned activities; they never got a phone call, for the successive events. This did not sit well with my father. He is not the type to repeat himself, over and over, about the same thing. At some point, he is going to take action. My sister continuously called my father to the house for discipline. He ruled his home with a firm hand.

My brother was moved a lot by this firm hand, as well. I don't know what my brother's problems were. He was doing things young boys do. His discipline started at a very young age, in elementary school. My father is adamant about children receiving an education, especially his own. My brother would not stop talking during school. My dad said, "Boy, close your mouth so you can learn that lesson. If you are talking in class, you are not able to learn anything; you prevent everyone around you from learning also." Every time report cards were issued, he would get a whipping. He would forget to do his chores; my brother would fall asleep or something. My father would go into his room and whip him; whip him up-out, of his sleep. My brother would forget to take out the trash. My dad would tell him, "Hey boy, don't you keep forgetting to take out that trash." Dad said, "It's wintertime son, go outside and rake up all the leaves in the yard." My brother went outside to clear the lawn. Approximately 15 minutes later, my brother came back inside holding the broken rake. My father yelled, "Boy, you broke that rake on purpose; just so you wouldn't have to do the yard! I'm not buying another one! You trying to be slick and you out-slicked yourself! You'd better get back out there and rake up those leaves with your hands!" He went back out to rake with his hands; he also took the broken rake. My brother was my little man so I would help him out as much as I could.

They were always being chastised, in one form or another. As for me, I rarely got any whippings. There was never any wiggle room for me to mess up. My sister and brother kept my parents on their toes. My discipline mostly came in the form of threats; delivered through gritted teeth. When I was in high school, I missed curfew. The harsh, verbal backlash brought tears to my eyes. I only needed to be told once. I felt that as long as he kept talking to me then I'd be okay. After all, this was my first offense. I kept nodding my head and I just agreed with everything he was saying. It worked; I was spared from significant bodily injury. I never missed curfew again.

My childhood would have been perfect, had I been an only child. I never heard my parents argue unless it was about my sister or brother. I felt like I had to constantly monitor them. I was always checking my brother. I was always checking my sister. I was always telling them, "Ya'll know, ya'll better act right or daddy is gonna come home." My sister and brother just didn't seem to get it. I got it because I always saw them getting it. They had their own agendas. They didn't seem to be listening to me.

Finally, it dawned on me that my mother was snitching on all three of her children. From that point, I concerned myself with my affairs only. My mom always taught me to focus on my own business and whatever other people are doing, doesn't matter. When mom called, dad came running. He liked to go through the house, from top to bottom, with his own special spring cleaning. When he came home for disciplinary reasons, he didn't only address the current problem; no, that would've been too simple. He wanted to address the current problems, all unresolved past problems, and any unforeseen future problems that may occur.

I felt like I was living under a microscope; absolutely no wiggle room. Not only did I have to consider the current reason he may be coming home; I also had to consider which events are approaching. Is it close to report card time? Did

I do all my chores? Are the dishes squeaky clean or did I leave a grease spot?

My dad would ask, my mom, how each of us were doing. He would ask my mom, "How's Vanessa doing?" It did not matter who he was coming to check on; he always asked, "How's Vanessa doing?" I hated that. Don't check on me, all the time. Just come check on these crash dummies that keep requesting you. I was a teenage black girl. How was I supposed to stay focused and oriented to my tasks when I was surrounded by these two light-skinned siblings, who didn't follow the rules? I followed the rules because I was a compliant, black girl. I wanted my father to come home of his own volition. I loved my dad but if my mom had to call him; I never wanted to see him. Those circumstances were never good. My dad liked to talk to his children; just to see where their minds were, how they were thinking. My liberal conversation, with my father, was determined by his purpose of being home. If mom called on him; I would say as little as possible to convey my meaning. If he was home of his own free-will; I casually and cautiously conversed. It was torture being raised, in a home, with my sister and brother. I had to get out of that house. Thank God; my dad forced me to go to college.

My father's weapon of choice was anything. He didn't appear to be choosy. The closest item would suffice. He used belts, switches, electrical extension cords, leather dog straps and for my brother-his fist. My sister and brother debate over which one of them got it worse, when we were children. Both of them got it bad; I'm not even, in the running, in this debate. My sister got it more often but my brother got it worse. The one-hitter-quitter definitely clenched the debate, for me.

Since I'm 40 years old, I asked my dad if he thought he was abusive. He says, "No." If you follow the rules then your behavior directs his behavior. If you don't follow the rules then he disciplines you as he sees fit. Repeated misbehavior called for more severe punishments. If you couldn't follow house rules then get out of his house. He would tell any of his three children to get out. That may have been his favorite phrase. It was definitely the most used phrase.

One day, my dad spanked one of my cousins. She used to hang out with me and my sister when we were younger. I mention her because one day she was making prank phone calls, threatening, and cussing out people. My dad spanked her. It's been almost 30 years and that spanking is still fresh in her mind. I don't know how many kids my dad has spanked but she has an unbiased opinion. She might not call it a spanking. She might call it a beat-down. She remembers it like it happened yesterday. He made a lasting impression on her. We both still laugh about that until this very day. She said, "Girl, I remember when Uncle Tj whipped me. From that day on, I said to myself, Uncle Tj will never get a chance to whip me again." She really emphasized the word never. She sang the word, never, and pronounced it in distinct syllables. She enunciated the first syllable, excessively (neeeeee-ver).

My brother decided to ditch school one day. My family relocated back to Atlanta before my brother started high school. I was away at college, so I heard about it. He left school and got on the city bus to go somewhere. After he got to his destination, he got off the bus. There was my father, stopped behind the bus. I think my dad drove him back to school. My mom told me, later, "That was divine intervention; something was about to happen to that boy." I responded, "What are the odds of dad being on that one street in Atlanta; forced to stop behind the one bus he was on, ditching?" I would have given anything to see his face when he locked eyes with my dad.

Since my mom has passed, I wished I had written down everything she told me. If I stored all this in a room; I would have a room full of repeated words. She said the same thing, redundantly, in her unique way. I can still talk with my dad. He once told me, "The only thing I ever learned; I learned from Brenda." I chuckled when he told me that. I thought to myself, "How many times did it take my mother to repeat those words to him, until he learned his lessons?" She was a very patient woman.

Traditional
Black Woman

WHEN I WRITE OF THE traditional black woman, I am talking about the ebony skin that was in Africa. Black people were the first people on earth. African people were traded into slavery. I read or heard, somewhere, these black slave traders only traded or sold their tribal enemies. They never sold any of their family or close loved ones. That makes sense to me. I'm not sure about the specifics of the trading.

Who were these people that were taken from their motherland? I am fascinated with the original black faces. What were the customs, habits, and characteristics of these people? I like the features of black people. I like the overall physiques' of black people. Black women have thick lips and supersize hips. Black men have a natural, muscular build. This ebony skin is precious to me because it is rare. I think the most beautiful black skin would be pitch-black skin. I have seen very black people, but I don't think I have ever seen anyone that is pitch-black. When I see dark people, I compare their skin color to a pitch-black tennis shoe (I compare white people with a white tennis shoe). Some blacks have come very close, but I have never seen anyone with truly black skin. I believe the skin that I am looking for may be extinct. I have never seen anyone as black as a tennis shoe. Every black person thinks their black is unique; for me, that pitch-black is what is precious and rare.

When black people were traded from Africa, half-white babies were being born. The American black face started to change. That face would never be the same again.

I don't know much about this group that composed the original people. I am very much interested. I've heard a lot about their struggles. I wonder what the black woman was like. What kind of strength did it take to endure the hardships ahead of her? Did she know that her offspring would fight for their freedom, for the rest of their lives?

Whether they ever regained their freedom or not; did she know they would always pursue it? Did she know this, pursuit for freedom, would be innate?

I wonder what the black man was like. What was it like to see black women degraded and disrespected? Horrible atrocities were committed. The original black woman had her man with her. Black people had to stick together because they were all they had. There was no time for distention among the group; with an entire race of people constantly attacking you. Black men supported their black women to weather them through the storm. There's that sexy trait again.

The black people, of this time period, constantly kept themselves uplifted; even in the time of adversity. With each negative comment endured, they had to stay positive. They used positive affirmations on a regular basis, probably millions of affirmations. This was a period of time when dark ebony faces were in large numbers. The children, of this time, received solace from those faces. If I made a black-face continuum; ebony faces still made up the majority on the continuum scale.

Black American Woman

ALL AMERICAN BLACK PEOPLE FIT in this group. Different variations of color compose Black America: black, dark brown, toffee, cocoa, light brown, mocha, light-yellow, caramel, high-yellow, etc. I would also include any person with a trace of black blood in this group. This category represents all the different skin tones of the black race.

Black people have gotten along for centuries. Black people used to stick together and support one another. Now, we can't seem to get along. Several issues need to be addressed because black people need to get it together.

Let's discuss the origin of the term "nigger". I am not racist; I am writing about historical facts. It is fact, the term "nigger" originated in England. The term "nigger" was used by white people to describe other white people. The term "nigger" was used to describe England's undesirables. The murderers, robbers, and rapist were the undesirable people who lived in England. These white people, in England; were raising sand, getting drunk, and shooting guns. The elite society, of England, wanted to get these undesirable people out of their land. The elite group decided to ship their undesirable people to America. When they arrived in America, white people did not like the word "nigger", which was assigned to them. White people, later, enslaved black people in America. White people decided to transfer their word "nigger" onto black people. From then on, white people called black people "nigger".

This word "nigger" is now being used within the black race. Why? Get that word out of the black race. Leave that word where it belongs, with the white race. The term "nigger" was not for us, by us; the term "nigger" is for them, by them. The term "nigger" was not originated to describe black people. That term has no place among the black group. Black people were descendants of kings, queens, and pharaohs; not ousted killers and hell-raisers. Black people were not from undesirables.

For some reason, the word "nigger" is in heavy rotation among the black group. Ironically, black people will use this word "nigger" to greet their closest friends and loved ones. They continuously insult those they love, the most. I have heard black people explain, "I only use that word with my homies or my best friends." Black people have told me, "it is not insulting because I don't use "nigger" with the "er"; I replace the "er" with an "a", to make it "nigga"." Somehow, using the word "nigga" instead of "nigger" is supposed to be honorable. However it is used, it is disrespectful. The word "nigger" should be eliminated from language, due to the negative connotation and history.

Just to throw in a male perspective, I asked my dad what he thought about the variation of the word "nigger"; dropping the "er" and adding the "a". My dad said, "Sounds to me like black folks are just trying to make-up a word." (ha ha, he's funny). He also said, "Black people aren't free, they are locked up in jail; and all those black people are in jail, using the word "nigga"." He is correct about that. Let me tell you about my experience.

I used to work at a secure facility in Oklahoma. It was not a jail. This facility is now closed. It was a state facility that housed and rehabilitated juvenile delinquents, youthful offenders, and young sex offenders. The staff, collectively, referred to all these kids as "the boys". These boys could be a handful. This place was a great facility. The staff really put forth a concerted effort to assist these juveniles. This wasn't the best facility but it was all they had. The boys used to tell me, "The only thing we learn here is how to be a better criminal."

The majority of these boys started, out in life, at a disadvantage. Other boys made bad decisions and started hanging with the wrong crowd and got into trouble. In life, we all have choices. If they did not work the program, things did not look good for them. This place had a lot of great things to offer. The boys just didn't take full advantage of the programs. These were teenage boys with criminal and delinquent minds. Their number one goal: manipulate staff and get all of your friends to manipulate staff. Just when you thought you could relax around these boys; that's when the real action was about to start. They brought challenges, in full measure, on a daily basis.

I learned a lot of great things at this facility. I still use some of their terms and concepts. One of their phrases: Don't be a crash dummy. This means, if you see one of your peers crashing (acting a fool), then don't fall into their negativity. Every juvenile, at this facility, was to offer positive support and encouragement to his peers. If they were caught encouraging negative behavior among each other, there were consequences (sanctions, chores, write-ups, etc.). Another phrase this facility used: Keep the focus on the I. This means, no matter what someone may do, keep the focus on the I. I like this one because it reminds me of what my mom used to say, "Just worry about you and no one else."

Black people are in high population within the juvenile system. The boys liked to use the word "nigga". Black boys used the word "nigga". White boys used the word "nigga". Indian boys used the word "nigga". Latino boys used the word "nigga". They liked to use that word in the juvenile system, a lot. When I heard a boy say the word "nigga", I would write a booking slip and give a sanction. I would tell the juvenile, "Sir, the word nigga is not allowed; write 100 times, I will not use the word nigga." The juvenile responded, "Bitch, I'll beat yo' ass, if you write that booking slip. I told the juvenile to check to his room. He refused. I told him, "Please don't threaten me. Get out of my face. You are off-limits because you are too close to my person. Get, at least, 6 feet away; so that I can feel comfortable." I also said, "No, you will not get a booking slip; you will receive a major rule violation for threatening me. Please check yourself to your room."

At this point, I expected every boy within ear-range to fully support and back me. Some of the boys tried to talk to the inappropriate juvenile, to no effect. I was pleased with this group of boys, at least they attempted; they put forth an effort to persuade him to behave properly. Other kids said nothing; I'm okay with that, I'm content with silence. For the group of boys who laughed, I would make a mental note; they would get their write-ups, later. When a juvenile is crashing, it is extremely important for his peers to encourage him to behave appropriately. When other kids start to laugh, the inappropriate juvenile starts to feed into the negativity; he then has an audience, to entertain. If things were not brought under control, it could get progressively worse.

The upset boy stared me down, as a form of intimidation. He paced, back and forth; his hands were balled into fists. I grabbed the radio, "Security." I informed everyone to be in their rooms, by the time security arrives; or they will receive a major rule violation, for hindering orderly operations of the facility. The juveniles made their choices.

The juveniles would complain to their counselors. Actually, they would complain to anyone; that would do something about Ms. Wilson. Their counselors would tell them, "Keep the focus on the I. When you enter the discussion, have the mind-frame of I; not Ms. Wilson." The counselors would ask the juveniles, "Were you following the rules? How could your behavior have been more appropriate?"

The juveniles basically complained on anyone that would do write-ups; but they put me on the chopping block. They would tell me, "You're stupid, you're fat, and you're ugly." It got a lot worse than that. I asked the juveniles to call me by my name. They chose to call me other names. I know they all loved me. They loved me so much; they didn't know how to handle it. They didn't know how to channel the love, in a positive direction. They verbally attacked me, relentlessly. I still love them all. I hope they are well. Those boys were very fortunate to have this strong black woman working with them.

The family unit is extremely important. Children can avoid many dilemmas, if they were part of a functioning family unit. There is a direct correlation between a functioning family unit and reduced teenage pregnancy, drug usage, unhealthy relationships, etc. The list of problems plaguing the black community is lengthy. The topics addressed in this book are not all-inclusive.

Gangs are all over America. Gangs affect every race. Membership, into gangs, is increasing among males and females. I don't know much about gangs but I know they are problematic. The rival gangs fight over things like turf, respect, and colors. When I worked at the secure facility, the boys used to try to explain the codes and rules of their gangs. I was not able to grasp what they were explaining. It did not make sense to me. When the boys would talk to me, they would "put it on the set". No matter the discussion, if one of the boys "put it on the set", then they were very serious about a subject. When a gang member lies on the set, they call it "blowing up the set". My dad said, "Don't join gangs. People, in gangs, end up dead, maimed, or in the penitentiary." I would advise surrounding yourself among people who are headed on a constructive path. Gang members' paths do not look promising. If you spend time with those who are a bad influence, replace them with those who are a good influence. Find others' with something on the ball; something going for themselves. Idle time is the devil's playground. Get involved in productive activities. Join a school club, religious organization, sports team, or read a book. Staying busy, with positive things, allows no time for trouble. Replace bad habits with good habits; eventually you will practice good habits.

There is a fashion trend that originated in prisons and jails. It is taking the American black nation by storm. People think it is cool and trendy to wear their pants hanging off their' buttocks. This appearance started in jail as a way to gain "easy access". Inmates were in prison having sex with each other. For "easy access", the men would already have their pants down. Security guards and security cameras are strategically placed in these facilities. Time was of the essence. They did not want to fumble around with their pants. It was more convenient letting the pants hang loose, around their upper legs; not pull the pants up securely. This reduced the preparation time needed for sex. People in society are now sporting this jail-house trend. People tell me that it is the current style. People show up at the workplace with their pants hanging or sagging off their butts. This is not a professional look. In the workplace, dress and look the part. Dress appropriately and pull up those pants. Anytime you are in public, pull up those pants. Elevate your image. You are making a statement. Dad said, "If you are walking around with your pants hanging or sagging off your butt, it means, you are a faggot."

Education is the key to advancement and success. So many black children are dropping out of school and jeopardizing their futures. Gaining the discipline needed to acquire an education begins at home. Parents have to hold their kids accountable. Dad said, "Teachers are for teaching, not for raising your children. Teachers should not have to teach your children how to behave in school. It is the parents' responsibility to get the child to school. It is the parents' responsibility to prepare and teach the child proper behavior, before arriving to school. Your child is supposed to know how to act before they get to school. The teacher can then deliver the lesson, uninterrupted; stopping only for student questions and clearer understanding." He also said, "You need an education to take care of yourself and your family, without having to work hard. Use your brain instead of your brawn."

The main subjects in school (3 R's): reading, 'riting, and 'rithmetic. My mama taught me how to study. Reading is fun and it's fundamental. Sometimes, people read words without comprehending what is read. What's the point of reading material, if you don't understand it? The goal is to understand what is read. You may have to re-read the material several different times, for understanding. That's how I am. Some people can read information once and understand it. I have to read it over and over until I finally understand it. I may learn at a slower pace, but that's okay; as long as I learn it. Mama said, "If you don't understand, then read it over and over until you do. Eventually, the information will sink into your head or you will have it memorized." She also said, "If you need information about a topic, go to the library; get a book and read all about it."

'Riting (writing) should be legible for everyone to read. Handwriting should be clear, not sloppy. Mama said, "At all times, make sure you speak correct English; you write the same as you speak." Parents can get into a habit of speaking broken English around their children. The children acquire these habits at a period when they are impressionable. They should learn proper English before they learn broken English. They should learn the correct way before they learn the incorrect way. Parents should practice good habits, language, and behavior. Parents set the primary example. The children are in a learning stage and parents should assist the learning process.

'Rithmetic (arithmetic, math). Mama said, "There's only one way to learn math. Open your math book, get out a blank sheet of paper, and work the math problems. Repeatedly, solve the math equations. If you don't understand how to work it, continue to go through the motions; systematically following the steps. After working so many of those math calculations, it's as if "a light comes on" in your head; you will finally get it. The more problems you work, the easier it becomes. Repetition is the key with math." People work the math problem. School work is exactly like learning a new rap song on the cd. You repeat it over and over until you learn it. Practice makes perfect.

I don't know what is going on with the music. I remember when music used to be good. I asked my dad what he thinks about music. Daddy said, "Ain't no mo' music. Music is gone. It is non-existent." He also explained, "When I was a young boy, in the 1950's, the music was always good. In the 1960's and 1970's, a new hit came out on the radio every week; especially in the 70's." Now he is 65 years old, he said, "I never thought I would still be hearing music, on the radio, from when I was a little boy. It still sounds good too. They are still playing that old music because today's music is unfortunate; music is gone. They have no talent; they are mad and upset. Due to their frustration, they start cussing, saying "nigga", and disrespecting their parents in the songs. What happened to music? Don't write a bunch of words in a song that mean nothing. Teach someone with your words." I explained to my Dad, "In the 1980's and 1990's music was still good, because I used to jam and dance to it. He responded, "That was when music started going down. There were some good rappers. When the old rappers left or died, that's when music went to hell." My dad likes the women artists better.

Tattoos and piercings are all the rage. Many people have tattoos and piercings, many don't. People have tattoos in observable areas: face, neck, arms, etc. Some of the tattoos are colored so it draws even more attention. I have seen people with piercings in the nose, eyebrows, lip, etc. Tattoos and piercings, in observable areas, severely interfere with gainful employment. My dad said, "Tattoos are for thugs, gangsters, and rich people. The rich people have their money, so they are doing their own thing. All of these rich people, that are on television, tatted-up with tattoos. These artists, actors, and sports figures are already rich; they are not seeking employment. As for the thugs and gangsters, they won't be contributing to society in a positive manner anyway." I advise not getting tattoos. Make sure your tattoos are not noticeable to others. I don't understand why people get tattoos. I think they get tattoos because they desperately want attention from others. Dad said, "They get tattoos because they are crazy and they have a mental problem."

As I go through everyday life, I have observed black people interacting with one another. I thought that the dark skin vs. light skin issue was diminishing but it seems that with every new generation, this issue continues to flare up all over again. What's the underlying problem? This issue reignites, with more intensity, with each generation that is added to the black race. This dark skin, light skin problem also exists among the black male population. The problem becomes more apparent among black women because women bicker.

If black people were all one skin color, there would be no dark skin, light skin issue. We are no longer one color and the variation runs the full gamut of browns. The powers, that be, have already determined that "white is right". Anyone that skews from white, will have a hard-time in society. Eventually, they will experience racism. So far, that is how it has always been.

There are several mixed races that compose the black race. Of all the mixed races, none are more closely scrutinized than those who are mixed with white blood. My dad said, "Those who are mixed, with black blood and white blood, should have the ability to maneuver around within each race. Those are the cards they are dealt. They are both black and white." This is my observation. As a whole, the white race has never received these mixed people who look black. The black race has not received these mixed people who look white. There is always resistance at some level.

I remember girls arguing about dark skin, light skin when I was a teenager. As the years passed, the topic dwindled. It didn't vanish, it decreased slightly. Now, the topic has reared its ugly head again. Dark skinned black women started getting along with the browns and light skinned women of the black race. As they are working things out, there is a huge influx of more mixed people into the black race. These mixed-looking people are only added to the black race, even though they are white. Those who pass as white might be able to enter the white race. I imagine they would have problems entering the black race.

The present American black-face continuum does not have as many dark ebony faces, as it once had. There are a lot more browns and light skin. To make an analogy, I would compare the black-face change to an opened spigot. During slavery times, there were more dark skin people and the mixed people slowly trickled through the spigot. These mixed people have always oriented toward the black race. The white race has never accepted them. Now, with the race mixing, it seems that this spigot is fully opened and flowing. There have been mixed people since slavery but never in this large quantity. That means there are less dark faces in the pool and the faces become lighter.

I believe as faces of the black race change; it affects the dynamics of the black woman's support group. I think this is the root cause of the problem. Anytime a woman's support group is shaken, there is chaos. That is why there is continuous chaos among black women, because this group is constantly changing. The problem has never been fully resolved; then there is another huge influx of white faces.

Black women have always depended on those in the black community for support. Black women do not see women like themselves represented on magazine covers, in massive numbers. They do not see their faces on television, especially the darkest. The lighter skin tones are televised. Having a support group is important for black women because it is acceptance. They have a fortress within each other. No one has ever reached back to pull up black people. On the contrary, black people have been knocked down constantly. This community of support is a place for black women to fit in. This group is all she has ever had for validation. Usually, when black people are on television, the media delivers bad news. Despite the wider variety of people in America, when television personalities announce America's opinion about a specific topic, it reflects white America's opinion. By no means is the opinion representative of all in America. The media should include a more diverse gallery of "races" when reporting.

Since the faces are becoming lighter, where does that leave the darkest of black women and girls? Not only does she not receive any support from those outside of her group; the support within her group is also diminishing and changes to resemble the oppressor. As the look of her support network changes, the change is playing out emotionally among black women and they continue to feud.

I have witnessed black women arguing. In general, women are going to have disagreements. Often, the disagreement switches to the subject of race. An altercation might start just because the mixed-white girl has shown up around black people. I have heard a black woman tell the mixed-white woman, "We know you have been around your white people. Don't come back here thinking you are better than anyone. If you want to convince someone you're better, go convince your white people." The mixed-white woman stated, "I don't think I'm better than you." I have heard them exchange derogatory slurs. The black woman will call the mixed-white woman everything and she disrespects the white skin and the black skin. The mixed-white woman will call the black woman everything and she disrespects the black skin. The arguments can become very heated and intense. How can we expect the kids to get along when the adults aren't getting along?

The dispute is about racism, everyone in the black race is fed-up with racism. The dispute is not about how black people feel about each other; it is about how another race views members of the black race. Another race views this mixed-white person as more acceptable. No one can change how another person views someone. Members, of the black race, know that we are all equal in the group; no one is considered more precious than another member. Mixed people cannot change someone else's views on racism. Within the black race, black people set the standards of beauty and acceptance. In order for us to continue to get along, we are going to have to continue supporting one another.

We cannot argue, endlessly. This applies to black males also. Once we each consider what the other needs, we can sustain each other. Don't focus on how differently she/he may look or how accepted she/he may be from another race. Stay focused on how this mixed person is treating you. S/He too has experienced racism. Mixed people belong in the black group because they need acceptance. Where else can they go? The black race is for anyone that is black. Lift yourself up. After you are stable and strong, lift up someone else in the group. Black people have been supporting each other for centuries. Continue the status quo; continue to get along. Give each other compliments without abandon. Be supportive. Black people, stop arguing.

This book is not only for black people; it transcends any race and gender. It is for anyone with challenges in life. We will have to wait for God to relieve us from the problems of the world or we will have to wait for people to change. There will always be something to keep the world divided: racism, religion, body type, age, etc. Until then, parents teach your children. Prepare them for the harsh realities that the world will bring. Children stay strengthened and encouraged. Arm yourself with positivity. Bring everything in your arsenal to keep yourself fortified. Negative people are always near. Keep yourselves uplifted, no matter the hardships. Praise yourself ad libitum, to the amount desired or needed.

Printed in the United States
By Bookmasters